50 Delicious Soups from Abroad Recipes

By: Kelly Johnson

Table of Contents

- Pho (Vietnam)
- Tom Yum Goong (Thailand)
- Ramen (Japan)
- Borscht (Ukraine)
- Minestrone (Italy)
- Gazpacho (Spain)
- Sopa de Lima (Mexico)
- Miso Soup (Japan)
- Hot and Sour Soup (China)
- Mulligatawny (India)
- Harira (Morocco)
- French Onion Soup (France)
- Caldo Gallego (Spain)
- Avgolemono (Greece)
- Laksa (Malaysia/Singapore)
- Chowder (USA)
- Sancocho (Colombia/Dominican Republic)

- Pho Ga (Vietnam)
- Ciorbă de burtă (Romania)
- Clam Chowder (USA)
- Chupe de Camarones (Peru)
- Tom Kha Gai (Thailand)
- Menudo (Mexico)
- Minestra di Verdure (Italy)
- Pea Soup (Denmark)
- Khao Soi (Thailand)
- Suimono (Japan)
- Pappa al Pomodoro (Italy)
- Salmorejo (Spain)
- Kimchi Jjigae (South Korea)
- Lentejas (Spain)
- Tabbouleh Soup (Lebanon)
- Fesenjan (Iran)
- Zurek (Poland)
- Sopa de Ajo (Spain)
- Pörkölt (Hungary)

- Potage Parmentier (France)
- Goulash (Hungary)
- Soup Joumou (Haiti)
- Kharcho (Georgia)
- Fish Soup (Iceland)
- Black Bean Soup (Cuba)
- Gado-Gado Soup (Indonesia)
- Lamb Shank Soup (Jordan)
- Spicy Corn Soup (Mexico)
- Sopa de Fideo (Mexico)
- Baked Potato Soup (USA)
- Pea and Ham Soup (Australia)
- Sopa de Mariscos (Latin America)
- Chilled Cucumber Soup (Russia)

Pho (Vietnam)
Ingredients:

- 8 oz rice noodles
- 1 lb beef (brisket, flank steak) or chicken (optional)
- 4 cups beef or chicken broth
- 1 onion, halved
- 2-3 slices ginger
- 3-4 cloves garlic, smashed
- 2-3 star anise
- 1 cinnamon stick
- 1 tbsp fish sauce
- 1 tbsp soy sauce
- 1 tsp sugar
- Fresh herbs (cilantro, basil)
- Lime wedges
- Bean sprouts
- Chili slices or hoisin sauce (optional for garnish)

Instructions:

1. Prepare the rice noodles according to the package instructions. Drain and set aside.

2. In a large pot, char the onion and ginger over an open flame or in a dry pan until blackened.

3. Add the onion, ginger, garlic, star anise, and cinnamon stick to the broth. Simmer for 30-45 minutes.

4. Remove the solids from the broth and strain it. Add fish sauce, soy sauce, and sugar to season.

5. Add the cooked noodles to a bowl and pour the hot broth over them.

6. Top with thinly sliced beef or chicken, herbs, lime wedges, bean sprouts, and chili slices or hoisin sauce.

7. Serve hot.

Tom Yum Goong (Thailand)
Ingredients:

- 4 cups chicken broth
- 1/2 lb shrimp, peeled and deveined
- 2-3 stalks lemongrass, smashed
- 4-5 kaffir lime leaves, torn
- 3-4 slices galangal (or ginger)
- 2-3 Thai bird's eye chilies, smashed
- 1-2 tbsp fish sauce
- 1 tbsp sugar
- 1 tbsp lime juice
- 1/2 cup mushrooms, sliced
- Fresh cilantro for garnish

Instructions:

1. In a pot, bring the chicken broth to a boil. Add lemongrass, lime leaves, galangal, and chilies.
2. Simmer for 5-10 minutes to infuse the flavors.
3. Add the shrimp and mushrooms to the broth, cooking for 2-3 minutes until the shrimp turn pink.
4. Season with fish sauce, sugar, and lime juice.
5. Remove from heat and discard the lemongrass, lime leaves, and galangal.

6. Garnish with cilantro and serve hot.

Ramen (Japan)
Ingredients:

- 8 oz ramen noodles
- 4 cups chicken or pork broth
- 1 tbsp soy sauce
- 1 tbsp miso paste
- 1 tbsp sesame oil
- 2 cloves garlic, minced
- 1 tsp grated ginger
- 1 boiled egg, halved
- 1/2 cup sliced green onions
- 1/2 cup cooked pork belly or chicken
- Nori (seaweed) for garnish
- Bamboo shoots and bean sprouts for garnish

Instructions:

1. Cook the ramen noodles according to package instructions. Drain and set aside.
2. In a pot, heat sesame oil over medium heat. Add garlic and ginger, sautéing for 1-2 minutes.
3. Add the chicken or pork broth, soy sauce, and miso paste. Simmer for 10 minutes.
4. Add the cooked noodles to the soup and stir.

5. Top with a boiled egg, sliced pork or chicken, green onions, nori, bamboo shoots, and bean sprouts.

6. Serve hot.

Borscht (Ukraine)
Ingredients:

- 1 lb beets, peeled and grated
- 1/2 cabbage, shredded
- 1 onion, chopped
- 1 carrot, chopped
- 1 potato, cubed
- 4 cups beef or vegetable broth
- 1 tbsp tomato paste
- 1 tbsp vinegar
- 1 tbsp sugar
- 2 tbsp olive oil
- 1-2 cloves garlic, minced
- Salt and pepper to taste
- Fresh dill for garnish
- Sour cream for garnish

Instructions:

1. In a large pot, heat olive oil over medium heat. Add the onion, carrot, and garlic. Sauté for 5-7 minutes until softened.

2. Add the grated beets, potatoes, cabbage, and broth. Bring to a boil, then reduce the heat and simmer for 30-40 minutes.

3. Stir in tomato paste, vinegar, sugar, salt, and pepper.

4. Simmer for an additional 10 minutes to allow the flavors to meld.

5. Serve with a dollop of sour cream and garnish with fresh dill.

Minestrone (Italy)
Ingredients:

- 4 cups vegetable broth
- 1 onion, chopped
- 2 cloves garlic, minced
- 1 carrot, chopped
- 1 celery stalk, chopped
- 1 zucchini, diced
- 1 can (14 oz) diced tomatoes
- 1 can (15 oz) kidney beans, drained
- 1 cup pasta (small shapes like ditalini)
- 1/2 cup spinach or kale, chopped
- 1 tbsp olive oil
- Salt and pepper to taste
- Fresh basil or parsley for garnish

Instructions:

1. In a large pot, heat olive oil over medium heat. Add the onion, carrot, celery, and garlic. Sauté for 5-7 minutes.
2. Add the zucchini, tomatoes, and vegetable broth. Bring to a boil.
3. Add the pasta and beans. Reduce the heat and simmer for 15-20 minutes until the pasta is tender.

4. Stir in spinach or kale and cook for an additional 2-3 minutes.

5. Season with salt and pepper to taste, and serve with fresh basil or parsley.

Gazpacho (Spain)
Ingredients:

- 4 tomatoes, chopped
- 1 cucumber, peeled and chopped
- 1 bell pepper, chopped
- 1/2 onion, chopped
- 2 cloves garlic, minced
- 2 tbsp olive oil
- 2 tbsp red wine vinegar
- 1 cup tomato juice
- Salt and pepper to taste
- Fresh basil or parsley for garnish

Instructions:

1. In a blender or food processor, combine the tomatoes, cucumber, bell pepper, onion, and garlic.
2. Blend until smooth.
3. Add olive oil, red wine vinegar, tomato juice, salt, and pepper. Blend again to combine.
4. Chill in the refrigerator for 2-3 hours before serving.
5. Serve cold, garnished with fresh basil or parsley.

Sopa de Lima (Mexico)

Ingredients:

- 4 cups chicken broth
- 1/2 lb chicken breast, cooked and shredded
- 1 onion, chopped
- 2 cloves garlic, minced
- 2 tomatoes, chopped
- 2 limes, juiced
- 1 tsp cumin
- 1 tsp oregano
- 1/4 cup cilantro, chopped
- Tortilla strips for garnish

Instructions:

1. In a pot, heat olive oil over medium heat. Add onion, garlic, and tomatoes. Sauté until softened.
2. Add the chicken broth, shredded chicken, cumin, and oregano. Simmer for 15 minutes.
3. Stir in lime juice and cilantro.
4. Serve the soup topped with tortilla strips.

Miso Soup (Japan)

Ingredients:

- 4 cups dashi (Japanese soup stock)
- 2 tbsp miso paste
- 1/2 cup tofu, cubed
- 2 tbsp seaweed (wakame)
- 2 green onions, chopped

Instructions:

1. In a pot, bring dashi to a boil.
2. Add miso paste and stir until dissolved.
3. Add tofu and seaweed, simmer for 2-3 minutes.
4. Garnish with green onions and serve.

Hot and Sour Soup (China)
Ingredients:

- 4 cups chicken or vegetable broth
- 1/2 cup mushrooms, sliced
- 1/2 cup bamboo shoots, sliced
- 1/4 cup tofu, cubed
- 2-3 tbsp soy sauce
- 1-2 tbsp rice vinegar
- 1 tsp chili paste
- 1 tsp sesame oil
- 1 egg, beaten
- 1/4 cup green onions, chopped
- Cornstarch for thickening (optional)

Instructions:

1. In a pot, bring the broth to a boil.
2. Add the mushrooms, bamboo shoots, tofu, soy sauce, rice vinegar, chili paste, and sesame oil.
3. Simmer for 5-7 minutes.
4. Slowly drizzle in the beaten egg, stirring gently.
5. Thicken with cornstarch if desired.

6. Garnish with green onions and serve.

Mulligatawny (India)
Ingredients:

- 4 cups chicken or vegetable broth
- 1 onion, chopped
- 2 cloves garlic, minced
- 1 tbsp curry powder
- 1 carrot, chopped
- 1 apple, chopped
- 1 cup lentils
- 1/2 cup coconut milk
- Salt and pepper to taste

Instructions:

1. In a pot, heat olive oil over medium heat. Add onion, garlic, and curry powder. Sauté until fragrant.
2. Add the carrot, apple, lentils, and broth. Bring to a boil, then reduce to a simmer for 25-30 minutes until lentils are tender.
3. Stir in coconut milk and season with salt and pepper.
4. Serve hot.

Harira (Morocco)

Ingredients:

- 4 cups vegetable broth
- 1/2 lb lamb, cubed
- 1 onion, chopped
- 2 cloves garlic, minced
- 2 tomatoes, chopped
- 1 tsp turmeric
- 1 tsp cumin
- 1/2 tsp cinnamon
- 1/4 cup cilantro, chopped
- 1/4 cup parsley, chopped
- 1/4 cup chickpeas, cooked
- 1/4 cup lentils
- 1 tbsp flour (optional)

Instructions:

1. In a pot, sauté lamb, onion, garlic, and spices for 5-7 minutes.
2. Add the tomatoes, broth, chickpeas, and lentils. Simmer for 30-40 minutes until everything is tender.
3. If desired, thicken the soup by stirring in a mixture of flour and water.

4. Garnish with cilantro and parsley.

5. Serve hot.

French Onion Soup (France)
Ingredients:

- 4 large onions, thinly sliced
- 4 cups beef broth
- 1/4 cup white wine
- 2 tbsp butter
- 1 tbsp olive oil
- 1 tsp thyme
- 1 baguette, sliced
- 1 cup Gruyère cheese, grated

Instructions:

1. In a large pot, heat butter and olive oil over medium heat. Add the onions and sauté until caramelized, about 25 minutes.
2. Add the white wine and simmer for 5 minutes.
3. Add the beef broth and thyme. Simmer for 15-20 minutes.
4. Ladle the soup into oven-safe bowls, top with a slice of baguette, and sprinkle with cheese.
5. Broil the soup in the oven until the cheese is melted and bubbly.
6. Serve hot.

Caldo Gallego (Spain)

Ingredients:

- 1 lb collard greens or turnip greens, chopped
- 1/2 lb chorizo, sliced
- 1/2 lb potatoes, peeled and diced
- 1/2 lb white beans (soaked overnight)
- 4 cups chicken or vegetable broth
- 2 cloves garlic, minced
- 1 onion, chopped
- 2 tbsp olive oil
- Salt and pepper to taste

Instructions:

1. In a large pot, heat olive oil over medium heat. Add the chorizo and cook until browned.
2. Add the garlic and onion, sauté for 5 minutes until softened.
3. Add the potatoes, beans, and broth. Bring to a boil and simmer for 30 minutes, until the potatoes and beans are tender.
4. Add the chopped greens and simmer for another 10 minutes until the greens are tender.
5. Season with salt and pepper to taste. Serve hot.

Avgolemono (Greece)
Ingredients:

- 4 cups chicken broth
- 2 eggs
- 1/4 cup lemon juice
- 1/4 cup rice
- 1/2 cup cooked chicken (optional)
- Salt and pepper to taste

Instructions:

1. Bring the chicken broth to a simmer in a pot. Add rice and cook until tender (about 15 minutes).
2. In a separate bowl, whisk together the eggs and lemon juice until smooth.
3. Slowly ladle some hot broth into the egg mixture, whisking constantly to temper the eggs.
4. Gradually add the egg mixture back into the simmering broth while stirring.
5. Add the cooked chicken, if using, and season with salt and pepper.
6. Serve warm.

Laksa (Malaysia/Singapore)

Ingredients:

- 4 cups chicken or vegetable broth
- 200g rice noodles
- 1/2 lb cooked shrimp
- 1/4 cup coconut milk
- 2 tbsp red curry paste
- 1 tbsp fish sauce
- 1 tbsp sugar
- 1-2 tbsp lime juice
- 2 boiled eggs, halved
- Fresh cilantro, mint, and bean sprouts for garnish

Instructions:

1. Cook the rice noodles according to the package instructions, then drain and set aside.
2. In a pot, bring the broth to a boil. Add the red curry paste, coconut milk, fish sauce, sugar, and lime juice.
3. Simmer for 5-10 minutes to combine the flavors.
4. Add the cooked shrimp and noodles. Stir to combine and heat through.
5. Serve in bowls, garnished with boiled eggs, fresh herbs, and bean sprouts.

Chowder (USA)
Ingredients:

- 4 cups chicken or vegetable broth
- 2 cups heavy cream
- 2 cups potatoes, peeled and diced
- 1/2 cup onion, chopped
- 1 cup corn kernels (fresh or frozen)
- 1/2 lb bacon, diced
- 2 cloves garlic, minced
- 1 tbsp butter
- Salt and pepper to taste

Instructions:

1. In a pot, cook the bacon over medium heat until crispy. Remove and set aside.
2. Add butter to the pot, then sauté the onion and garlic until soft (about 5 minutes).
3. Add the potatoes, broth, and cream. Bring to a boil, then reduce to a simmer for 20-25 minutes, until the potatoes are tender.
4. Add the corn and cook for an additional 5-7 minutes.
5. Season with salt and pepper. Serve topped with crispy bacon.

Sancocho (Colombia/Dominican Republic)

Ingredients:

- 1 lb chicken, pork, or beef (with bones)
- 4 cups water
- 3-4 potatoes, peeled and chopped
- 2 ears of corn, cut into pieces
- 2 plantains, peeled and chopped
- 2 carrots, chopped
- 1 onion, chopped
- 2 cloves garlic, minced
- 1 tsp cumin
- 1 tsp oregano
- Salt and pepper to taste
- Fresh cilantro for garnish

Instructions:

1. In a large pot, combine the meat and water. Bring to a boil, then reduce the heat and simmer for 1-2 hours, until the meat is tender.
2. Add the potatoes, corn, plantains, carrots, onion, garlic, cumin, and oregano.
3. Simmer for an additional 30 minutes, until the vegetables are tender.
4. Season with salt and pepper to taste.

5. Garnish with fresh cilantro and serve hot.

Pho Ga (Vietnam)

Ingredients:

- 4 cups chicken broth
- 1 lb chicken (whole or thighs)
- 8 oz rice noodles
- 1 onion, halved
- 2-3 slices ginger
- 1 tbsp fish sauce
- 1 tbsp soy sauce
- 1 tsp sugar
- Fresh herbs (cilantro, basil)
- Lime wedges
- Bean sprouts and chili slices for garnish

Instructions:

1. Bring the chicken broth to a boil in a large pot. Add the onion, ginger, fish sauce, soy sauce, and sugar. Simmer for 30 minutes.
2. Add the chicken to the pot and cook for 15-20 minutes, until fully cooked.
3. Remove the chicken, shred the meat, and set aside.
4. Cook the rice noodles according to package instructions, then divide into bowls.
5. Pour the hot broth over the noodles and top with shredded chicken, fresh herbs, lime wedges, and garnishes.

Ciorbă de Burtă (Romania)

Ingredients:

- 2 lbs beef tripe, cleaned and cut into strips
- 1 lb beef bones
- 10 cups water
- 2 onions, chopped
- 2 carrots, chopped
- 2 cloves garlic, minced
- 1 bay leaf
- 2 tbsp vinegar
- 2 eggs, beaten
- 1/2 cup sour cream
- Salt and pepper to taste
- Fresh parsley for garnish

Instructions:

1. In a large pot, combine the beef bones and water. Bring to a boil, then reduce the heat and simmer for 2-3 hours.

2. Add the beef tripe, onions, carrots, garlic, and bay leaf. Simmer for another 1-2 hours until the tripe is tender.

3. Add vinegar, salt, and pepper to taste.

4. Mix the sour cream and eggs in a bowl, then slowly add to the soup while stirring to avoid curdling.

5. Garnish with fresh parsley and serve hot.

Clam Chowder (USA)
Ingredients:

- 2 cups clams, shucked
- 4 cups chicken or vegetable broth
- 1 cup heavy cream
- 2 cups potatoes, peeled and diced
- 1/2 cup onion, chopped
- 1/4 cup celery, chopped
- 2 tbsp butter
- 2 cloves garlic, minced
- 1 tsp thyme
- Salt and pepper to taste
- Fresh parsley for garnish

Instructions:

1. In a large pot, heat butter over medium heat. Add the onion, celery, and garlic, sautéing until soft.

2. Add the potatoes and broth. Bring to a boil, then reduce to a simmer for 15-20 minutes until the potatoes are tender.

3. Add the clams and heavy cream. Simmer for 5 minutes.

4. Season with thyme, salt, and pepper to taste.

5. Garnish with fresh parsley and serve hot.

Chupe de Camarones (Peru)

Ingredients:

- 1 lb shrimp, peeled and deveined
- 4 cups fish stock or water
- 2 cups potatoes, peeled and diced
- 1/2 cup corn kernels (fresh or frozen)
- 1/2 cup rice
- 1/2 cup milk
- 1 tbsp aji amarillo (yellow chili paste)
- 1/2 cup queso fresco (fresh cheese)
- Fresh cilantro for garnish

Instructions:

1. In a pot, bring the fish stock to a boil. Add the potatoes, corn, and rice. Simmer for 20 minutes until the vegetables are tender.
2. Add the shrimp and cook until pink, about 3-4 minutes.
3. Stir in the milk and aji amarillo.
4. Top with queso fresco and fresh cilantro.
5. Serve hot.

Tom Kha Gai (Thailand)

Ingredients:

- 4 cups chicken broth
- 1 lb chicken, sliced thin
- 1 can (14 oz) coconut milk
- 2-3 stalks lemongrass, smashed
- 3-4 kaffir lime leaves, torn
- 3-4 slices galangal (or ginger)
- 2-3 Thai bird's eye chilies, smashed
- 2 tbsp fish sauce
- 1 tbsp sugar
- 1 tbsp lime juice
- Fresh cilantro for garnish

Instructions:

1. In a pot, bring the chicken broth to a boil. Add the lemongrass, lime leaves, galangal, and chilies.
2. Simmer for 5-10 minutes to infuse the flavors.
3. Add the chicken and coconut milk, simmer for 15-20 minutes.
4. Stir in the fish sauce, sugar, and lime juice.
5. Garnish with fresh cilantro and serve hot.

Menudo (Mexico)
Ingredients:

- 2 lbs beef tripe, cleaned and cut into strips
- 1 lb beef shank or oxtail
- 2 cups hominy (canned or dried)
- 2 cloves garlic, minced
- 1 onion, chopped
- 1 tbsp dried oregano
- 2 tbsp chili powder
- 2 bay leaves
- 1 tsp cumin
- 1 tbsp apple cider vinegar
- 6 cups beef broth
- 1 lime, cut into wedges
- Fresh cilantro for garnish

Instructions:

1. In a large pot, combine the beef shank, tripe, hominy, garlic, onion, oregano, chili powder, bay leaves, cumin, and beef broth.
2. Bring to a boil, then reduce to a simmer and cook for 3-4 hours until the beef and tripe are tender.
3. Add vinegar and season with salt and pepper.

4. Serve hot, garnished with fresh cilantro and lime wedges.

Minestra di Verdure (Italy)

Ingredients:

- 1/2 lb mixed vegetables (carrots, celery, potatoes, zucchini)
- 1 onion, chopped
- 2 cloves garlic, minced
- 1 can (14 oz) diced tomatoes
- 1/4 cup pasta (small like ditalini or elbow macaroni)
- 4 cups vegetable broth
- 1/4 cup olive oil
- 1 tbsp fresh basil, chopped
- Salt and pepper to taste
- Fresh Parmesan cheese for garnish

Instructions:

1. Heat olive oil in a large pot and sauté the onion and garlic until soft.
2. Add the mixed vegetables and cook for 5 minutes.
3. Add the diced tomatoes, pasta, and vegetable broth. Bring to a boil, then reduce to a simmer and cook for 20 minutes.
4. Season with salt, pepper, and fresh basil.
5. Serve with grated Parmesan cheese.

Pea Soup (Denmark)
Ingredients:

- 1 lb split peas
- 1 ham hock or 1/2 lb ham, diced
- 4 cups vegetable or chicken broth
- 1 onion, chopped
- 2 carrots, diced
- 2 cloves garlic, minced
- 1 bay leaf
- 1 tsp dried thyme
- Salt and pepper to taste
- Fresh parsley for garnish

Instructions:

1. In a large pot, combine the peas, ham hock, onion, carrots, garlic, and broth.
2. Bring to a boil, then reduce to a simmer and cook for 1-2 hours until the peas are tender and the soup is thickened.
3. Remove the ham hock, shred the meat, and return it to the soup.
4. Season with thyme, salt, and pepper.
5. Garnish with fresh parsley and serve hot.

Khao Soi (Thailand)

Ingredients:

- 4 cups chicken broth
- 1 lb chicken (thighs or breast), cooked and shredded
- 1 can (14 oz) coconut milk
- 2 tbsp red curry paste
- 1 tbsp fish sauce
- 1 tbsp sugar
- 1-2 tbsp lime juice
- 8 oz egg noodles (or rice noodles)
- Fresh cilantro, onions, and lime wedges for garnish
- Crispy fried noodles for topping

Instructions:

1. Cook the noodles according to package instructions, then set aside.
2. In a pot, bring the chicken broth to a boil. Add the coconut milk, curry paste, fish sauce, sugar, and lime juice.
3. Simmer for 10 minutes to blend the flavors.
4. Add the shredded chicken and cooked noodles.
5. Serve the soup with fresh cilantro, onion, lime wedges, and crispy noodles.

Suimono (Japan)

Ingredients:

- 4 cups dashi broth
- 1/2 lb tofu, cubed
- 1/2 cup mushrooms (shiitake or enoki)
- 1/2 tsp soy sauce
- 1/4 tsp mirin
- 2 green onions, sliced
- Fresh cilantro for garnish

Instructions:

1. In a pot, bring the dashi broth to a simmer.
2. Add the tofu, mushrooms, soy sauce, and mirin.
3. Simmer for 5 minutes until the tofu is warmed and the mushrooms are tender.
4. Serve hot, garnished with sliced green onions and fresh cilantro.

Pappa al Pomodoro (Italy)

Ingredients:

- 4 cups vegetable or chicken broth
- 6 ripe tomatoes, chopped
- 2 cups day-old bread, torn into pieces
- 1 onion, chopped
- 2 cloves garlic, minced
- 2 tbsp olive oil
- 1 tsp fresh basil, chopped
- Salt and pepper to taste
- Fresh Parmesan cheese for garnish

Instructions:

1. Heat olive oil in a large pot. Add the onion and garlic and sauté until soft.
2. Add the tomatoes and cook for 10 minutes until they break down into a sauce.
3. Add the broth and bread, and simmer for 20 minutes, stirring occasionally.
4. Season with salt, pepper, and fresh basil.
5. Serve hot, topped with Parmesan cheese.

Salmorejo (Spain)

Ingredients:

- 6 ripe tomatoes
- 1/4 cup olive oil
- 2 slices day-old bread
- 1 clove garlic
- 1 tbsp red wine vinegar
- Salt to taste
- 2 hard-boiled eggs, chopped for garnish
- Jamón ibérico (optional)

Instructions:

1. In a blender, combine the tomatoes, bread, garlic, olive oil, vinegar, and salt.
2. Blend until smooth.
3. Chill in the refrigerator for at least 1 hour.
4. Serve cold, topped with chopped hard-boiled eggs and jamón ibérico.

Kimchi Jjigae (South Korea)

Ingredients:

- 2 cups kimchi, chopped
- 1/2 lb pork (or tofu), sliced
- 4 cups beef or vegetable broth
- 2 cloves garlic, minced
- 1 tbsp gochujang (Korean chili paste)
- 2 tbsp soy sauce
- 1 onion, sliced
- 1/2 zucchini, sliced
- 1-2 green onions, chopped

Instructions:

1. In a pot, sauté the pork (or tofu) with garlic and gochujang until browned.
2. Add the kimchi, soy sauce, broth, onion, and zucchini.
3. Bring to a boil, then reduce to a simmer for 30-40 minutes.
4. Garnish with chopped green onions and serve hot.

Lentejas (Spain)

Ingredients:

- 1 lb lentils, rinsed
- 1/2 lb chorizo or sausage, sliced
- 4 cups vegetable or chicken broth
- 1 onion, chopped
- 2 cloves garlic, minced
- 2 carrots, diced
- 1 bay leaf
- 1 tsp paprika
- Salt and pepper to taste

Instructions:

1. In a large pot, sauté the chorizo, onion, garlic, and carrots until softened.
2. Add the lentils, broth, bay leaf, paprika, and salt.
3. Bring to a boil, then reduce to a simmer and cook for 1-1.5 hours until the lentils are tender.
4. Season with pepper and serve hot.

Tabbouleh Soup (Lebanon)

Ingredients:

- 4 cups vegetable broth
- 1/2 cup bulgur wheat
- 1/2 cup fresh parsley, chopped
- 1/4 cup fresh mint, chopped
- 2 tomatoes, diced
- 1/2 cucumber, diced
- 1/4 cup lemon juice
- Salt and pepper to taste

Instructions:

1. In a small bowl, soak the bulgur wheat in warm water for 15 minutes, then drain.
2. In a pot, bring the broth to a boil. Add the soaked bulgur wheat and simmer for 10 minutes.
3. Add the parsley, mint, tomatoes, cucumber, lemon juice, salt, and pepper.
4. Simmer for an additional 5-10 minutes, then serve hot or chilled.

Fesenjan (Iran) – Persian Pomegranate Walnut Stew

Ingredients:

- 1 lb chicken thighs or duck, cut into pieces
- 1 large onion, finely chopped
- 1 ½ cups walnuts, ground
- 2 cups chicken broth
- 1 cup pomegranate molasses
- 1 tbsp sugar (optional)
- 1/2 tsp cinnamon
- Salt and pepper to taste
- 2 tbsp oil

Instructions:

1. Sauté onions in oil until golden. Add chicken, salt, and pepper. Brown lightly.
2. Stir in ground walnuts and cook for 5 minutes.
3. Add broth, bring to a boil, then reduce to a simmer. Cover and cook for 30 minutes.
4. Stir in pomegranate molasses and cinnamon. Simmer for another 30–40 minutes until thick.
5. Adjust sweetness with sugar. Serve with saffron rice.

Żurek (Poland) – Sour Rye Soup

Ingredients:

- 1 cup sour rye starter (zakwas) or 1 cup rye flour + 1 cup warm water + 2 garlic cloves (ferment for 3 days)
- 1/2 lb smoked sausage, sliced
- 1 onion, chopped
- 2 garlic cloves, minced
- 1 bay leaf
- 4 cups broth
- 1/2 cup sour cream
- 2 boiled eggs, halved
- Salt and pepper to taste
- 1 tsp marjoram

Instructions:

1. Sauté onion and garlic, add broth, bay leaf, sausage, and marjoram. Simmer for 20 minutes.
2. Add the sour rye starter and simmer another 10 minutes.
3. Stir in sour cream slowly to avoid curdling.
4. Serve hot with boiled eggs and rye bread.

Sopa de Ajo (Spain) – Garlic Soup

Ingredients:

- 6 garlic cloves, sliced
- 4 cups chicken or vegetable broth
- 4 slices stale bread
- 2 eggs
- 1 tsp smoked paprika
- Olive oil
- Salt and pepper to taste

Instructions:

1. Heat olive oil in a pan. Fry garlic until fragrant.
2. Add paprika, then immediately add broth and bread.
3. Simmer 10 minutes until bread softens.
4. Crack in the eggs and poach for 3–4 minutes.
5. Serve with a drizzle of olive oil and crusty bread.

Pörkölt (Hungary) – Paprika Stew

Ingredients:

- 1.5 lbs beef chuck, cubed
- 2 onions, finely chopped
- 2 tbsp sweet Hungarian paprika
- 2 garlic cloves, minced
- 1 green bell pepper, chopped
- 1 tomato, chopped
- 1 ½ cups beef broth
- Salt and pepper to taste
- Oil

Instructions:

1. Sauté onions in oil until golden. Remove from heat and stir in paprika.
2. Return to heat, add beef, garlic, salt, and pepper. Brown meat.
3. Add bell pepper, tomato, and broth. Simmer, covered, for 1.5–2 hours.
4. Serve with nokedli (spaetzle) or boiled potatoes.

Potage Parmentier (France) – Leek and Potato Soup

Ingredients:

- 3 large leeks (white parts only), sliced
- 3 medium potatoes, diced
- 1 onion, chopped
- 4 cups vegetable or chicken broth
- 2 tbsp butter
- Salt and pepper to taste
- Cream or crème fraîche (optional)

Instructions:

1. Sauté leeks and onions in butter until soft.
2. Add potatoes and broth, simmer 30 minutes.
3. Blend until smooth, season, and add cream if desired.
4. Serve with fresh chives or parsley.

Goulash (Hungary) – Hearty Beef Stew

Ingredients:

- 2 lbs beef chuck, cubed
- 2 onions, chopped
- 2 tbsp Hungarian paprika
- 2 garlic cloves, minced
- 2 carrots, sliced
- 1 green pepper, chopped
- 1 tomato, chopped
- 4 cups beef broth
- 1 tsp caraway seeds
- Salt and pepper

Instructions:

1. Sauté onions until golden. Stir in paprika, then add beef and brown.
2. Add garlic, vegetables, caraway, tomato, and broth.
3. Simmer for 2 hours until beef is tender.
4. Serve with crusty bread or noodles.

Soup Joumou (Haiti) – New Year's Pumpkin Soup

Ingredients:

- 1 lb beef stew meat
- 1 small pumpkin (or 2 cups pureed pumpkin)
- 2 carrots, diced
- 2 potatoes, diced
- 1 turnip, diced
- 1 stalk celery, diced
- 1 onion, chopped
- 2 garlic cloves
- 1 cup cabbage, chopped
- 1 scotch bonnet (optional)
- 1 tbsp lime juice
- Salt, pepper, thyme
- Pasta (e.g., macaroni or spaghetti)

Instructions:

1. Marinate beef with garlic, onion, thyme, lime juice. Brown and simmer with water until tender.
2. Add pumpkin and boil until soft. Purée pumpkin, return to pot.
3. Add vegetables, pasta, and spices. Simmer until tender.

4. Serve hot as a symbol of freedom and resilience.

Kharcho (Georgia) – Spicy Beef and Walnut Soup

Ingredients:

- 1 lb beef, cubed
- 1 onion, chopped
- 2 cloves garlic
- 1/2 cup ground walnuts
- 1 tbsp tomato paste
- 1 tsp ground coriander
- 1/2 tsp fenugreek
- 1/2 tsp cinnamon
- 1 tbsp rice
- 4 cups beef broth
- Fresh cilantro
- Salt and chili flakes to taste

Instructions:

1. Cook beef with onions until browned. Add tomato paste, garlic, spices, and broth.
2. Simmer for 1 hour. Add rice, cook until tender.
3. Stir in ground walnuts and simmer another 10 minutes.
4. Garnish with fresh cilantro and serve hot.

Fish Soup (Iceland) – Fiskisúpa

Ingredients:

- 1 lb cod or haddock, cut into chunks
- 1 leek, sliced
- 1 onion, chopped
- 2 carrots, sliced
- 1 potato, diced
- 4 cups fish stock or water
- 1 cup cream
- 1 tbsp butter
- Salt, pepper, dill

Instructions:

1. Sauté onions, leeks, and carrots in butter.
2. Add potatoes and fish stock. Simmer until potatoes are soft.
3. Add fish, simmer 5–7 minutes.
4. Stir in cream, dill, salt, and pepper. Serve with rye bread.

Black Bean Soup (Cuba)

Ingredients:

- 2 cups dried black beans (or 3 cans, drained and rinsed)
- 1 onion, chopped
- 1 green bell pepper, chopped
- 3 cloves garlic, minced
- 1 tsp cumin
- 1 tsp oregano
- 1 bay leaf
- 4 cups vegetable or chicken broth
- 1 tbsp vinegar
- Salt and pepper to taste
- Olive oil

Instructions:

1. If using dried beans, soak overnight and simmer until tender.
2. Sauté onion, bell pepper, and garlic in olive oil. Add cumin and oregano.
3. Add beans, broth, bay leaf, and simmer 30–40 minutes.
4. Remove bay leaf, partially blend for creaminess.
5. Stir in vinegar, season to taste. Serve with rice or crusty bread.

Gado-Gado Soup (Indonesia-Inspired)

(Traditional Gado-Gado is a salad, but this is a soup interpretation.)

Ingredients:

- 1 can coconut milk
- 2 cups vegetable broth
- 1/2 cup peanut butter
- 1 tbsp soy sauce
- 1 garlic clove, minced
- 1 tsp ginger, grated
- 1 carrot, thinly sliced
- 1 handful green beans, halved
- 1 boiled egg per bowl
- Tofu or tempeh (optional)
- Lime wedges and crushed peanuts for garnish

Instructions:

1. Sauté garlic and ginger. Add broth, coconut milk, and peanut butter. Whisk until smooth.
2. Simmer carrots and green beans until tender.
3. Add tofu if using, and heat through.
4. Serve hot with a halved boiled egg, lime, and crushed peanuts.

Lamb Shank Soup (Jordan)

Ingredients:

- 2 lamb shanks
- 1 onion, chopped
- 2 carrots, chopped
- 1 tomato, chopped
- 1/2 cup rice or freekeh
- 1 tsp allspice
- 1 tsp cinnamon
- 1/2 tsp cardamom
- Salt and pepper to taste
- 6 cups water or broth
- Fresh parsley for garnish

Instructions:

1. Brown lamb shanks in a large pot. Remove and set aside.
2. Sauté onion, carrots, and tomato. Add spices and stir.
3. Return lamb, add broth. Simmer for 1.5–2 hours until lamb is tender.
4. Add rice or freekeh and cook until soft.
5. Serve hot with parsley and flatbread.

Spicy Corn Soup (Mexico)

Ingredients:

- 3 cups corn kernels (fresh or frozen)
- 1 small onion, chopped
- 1 garlic clove, minced
- 1 jalapeño, seeded and chopped
- 1 tsp cumin
- 4 cups vegetable broth
- 1/4 cup crema or sour cream
- Lime juice, cilantro, chili flakes for garnish

Instructions:

1. Sauté onion, garlic, and jalapeño. Add cumin and corn, cook 5 minutes.
2. Add broth and simmer for 15 minutes.
3. Blend partially for texture, stir in crema, adjust seasoning.
4. Serve with lime, cilantro, and chili flakes.

Sopa de Fideo (Mexico)

Ingredients:

- 1 cup fideo noodles (or broken vermicelli)
- 2 tomatoes, blended
- 1/4 onion
- 2 garlic cloves
- 4 cups chicken broth
- 1 tsp cumin
- 1 tbsp oil
- Salt to taste
- Lime and cilantro for garnish

Instructions:

1. Blend tomatoes, onion, and garlic until smooth.
2. Toast fideo noodles in oil until golden.
3. Add tomato mixture and cook 5 minutes.
4. Add broth and cumin, simmer until noodles are tender.
5. Serve with lime and chopped cilantro.

Baked Potato Soup (USA)

Ingredients:

- 4 baked potatoes, chopped
- 1/2 onion, chopped
- 2 cloves garlic
- 4 cups milk or broth
- 1/2 cup sour cream
- 1/2 cup shredded cheddar
- 1/4 cup chopped bacon (optional)
- Green onions for garnish
- Butter, salt, and pepper

Instructions:

1. Sauté onion and garlic in butter. Add chopped potatoes and mash slightly.
2. Stir in milk/broth and simmer until thickened.
3. Add sour cream, cheese, and bacon if using.
4. Season and serve with green onions and extra cheese.

Pea and Ham Soup (Australia)

Ingredients:

- 2 cups split peas
- 1 smoked ham hock or leftover ham
- 1 onion, chopped
- 1 carrot, diced
- 2 celery stalks, chopped
- 6 cups water or broth
- Bay leaf, thyme
- Salt and pepper

Instructions:

1. Combine all ingredients in a large pot. Bring to boil, reduce to simmer.
2. Cook for 2 hours until peas are soft and ham falls apart.
3. Remove ham, shred, and return to pot.
4. Season and serve with crusty bread.

Sopa de Mariscos (Latin America) – Seafood Soup

Ingredients:

- 1/2 lb shrimp
- 1/2 lb mussels or clams
- 1/2 lb white fish, cubed
- 1 tomato, chopped
- 1 onion, chopped
- 2 garlic cloves
- 4 cups seafood broth
- 1/2 cup coconut milk (optional)
- 1/2 tsp cumin
- Cilantro, lime, and chili flakes

Instructions:

1. Sauté onion, garlic, and tomato. Add cumin and broth.
2. Add fish, then shrimp and mussels. Simmer until cooked.
3. Stir in coconut milk if using. Season and garnish with lime and cilantro.

Chilled Cucumber Soup (Russia) – Okroshka Style

Ingredients:

- 2 cucumbers, diced
- 1 cup kefir or plain yogurt
- 1/2 cup water or sparkling mineral water
- 2 hard-boiled eggs, chopped
- 1 small potato, cooked and diced
- 2 tbsp dill, chopped
- Salt and pepper
- Squeeze of lemon

Instructions:

1. Mix kefir, water, salt, pepper, and lemon juice.
2. Add cucumber, potato, eggs, and dill.
3. Chill for 1–2 hours. Serve cold with rye bread.

www.ingramcontent.com/pod-product-compliance
Lightning Source LLC
LaVergne TN
LVHW081318060526
838201LV00055B/2351